A Stoic's Guide to Retirement

Embracing Serenity and Contentment

Table of Contents

Chapter 1. Introduction

Retirement is a phase of life that opens up vistas of boundless opportunities, yet can also bring with it substantial challenges. An answer to these challenges may surprisingly lie within the millennia-old philosophy of Stoicism. In the special report "A Stoic's Guide to Retirement: Embracing Serenity and Contentment," we explore this unique approach, viewing retirement through the lens of Stoic wisdom, providing insightful guidance to navigate through this new phase with fortitude and grace. This guide is not only set to redefine retirement but it will propel you to see it as an opportunity to cultivate peace, delight in the simple joys, and continue a journey of self-enlightenment. Dip in and out of this dynamic guide, weave in Stoic strategies into your everyday life, embrace your retirement as a time of serenity and contentment, and above all, transform the way you perceive this significant life stage. By the end of this report, you'll surely be thinking, "Retirement? Bring it on!"

Chapter 2. Introduction: Redefining Retirement through Stoicism

As we step onto the threshold of retirement, it is not uncommon to be assailed by a maelstrom of emotions - from joy and relief to apprehension and fear. How will we navigate this new territory, marked as it is by the ebb and flow of leisure and uncertainty? The ancient philosophy of Stoicism, renowned for its wisdom and ageless application to the vagaries of the human experience, provides us with a profound and unique compass.

Stoicism, a philosophy founded in the early 3rd century BC, teaches us to find serenity in acceptance, empowerment in focusing on what we can influence, and joy in the simple pleasures of life. Grounded in logic and observations of nature, Stoicism promotes the idea that we have the power to control our reactions to external events and circumstances. It tells us that external things are not good or bad but our thoughts about them make them so.

To redefine retirement through the lens of Stoicism is to transform it into a period of life replete with boundless opportunities and profound tranquility.

2.1. Stoicism: The Philosophy for Life's Seasons

Stoicism is no stranger to life's seasons. Principle Stoic philosophers like Seneca and Epictetus, were keen observers of life, providing us guidance across the spectrum of human experiences. They emphasized the importance of virtue, control over one's perceptions, and acceptance of the natural order of things. These teachings offer a wellspring of wisdom, cascading through time and space to help us redefine retirement.

We are taught by Stoicism that the natural order of things is not foul nor fair, but simply is. And since retirement is a part of the journey, an inevitable season in the calendar of life, it holds no predisposed negativity. It simply is. Seeing this natural transition through the lens of Stoicism helps us to redefine it from a potentially frightening or melancholic phase into a new era ripe with opportunities to embrace serenity and contentment.

2.2. The Stoic Virtues: A Guidepost for Retirement

In the realm of Stoicism, four cardinal virtues hold sway: Wisdom, Courage, Justice, and Temperance. These provide us with a moral compass and help us to direct our actions, thoughts, and perceptions. They guide us in flipping the script on retirement.

Wisdom, or practical knowledge, serves as our compass. It guides us to differentiate what is within our control and what is not—an important understanding to stave off unnecessary anxieties and fears that often accompany retirement.

Courage, the second virtue, is not just the bravery to face physical threats but the determination to confront fear, uncertainty, and shifting landscapes of life. It is directly applicable as we navigate retirement, encouraging us to step into unfamiliar territories with resilience and determination.

Practicing justice, or fairness, teaches us that our worth is not determined by our profession but by our character. In retirement, the lack of professional identity can be disconcerting. But Stoic philosophy encourages us to draw our identity from the virtue of justice and our ability to do good, reassuring us that this new phase of life does not diminish our worth.

Lastly, Temperance, or moderation, encourages us to indulge in pleasures, but not become a slave to them. This is imminently applicable for retirees, who now have ample time on hand, and can prevent them from falling into unhealthy patterns of excessive leisure activities or uncontrolled idleness.

2.3. Stoicism and the Pursuit of Serenity

One of the foundational ideals of Stoicism is the pursuit of 'Ataraxia', or serenity - an emotional state where one is free from distress and worry. This is achieved by focusing on the aspects of life within our control and maintaining a disciplined indifference towards those beyond our influence.

The flux of retirement - of income, daily routine, professional identity - can often seem vast and intimidating. But the Stoic concept of Ataraxia guides us to de-clutter our anxieties, focusing attention and efforts towards what we can influence and making peace with what we cannot.

For retirees, it is a consciousness of the passing time. By accepting our retiree status and focusing on the here and now, we begin to calm the raging sea of anxieties and irksome thoughts around faded youth or professional usefulness. We can start to appreciate every new dawn as a day brimming with possibilities rather than a canvass of regrets and lost opportunities.

2.4. Embracing Simplicity: Lessons from Stoicism

Stoicism propounds an affinity for the basic pleasures of life. It encourages us to derive joy from simple things - from the beauty of a sunrise to the warmth of a conversation. This most certainly does not adjourn us to a life of austerity but promotes an appreciation for life's simple pleasures.

As we move into retirement, the frenetic pace of life often slows down. This opens up the opportunity to take note of, enjoy, and be grateful for life's simple joys - be it spending time with loved ones, pursuing a hobby long forgotten, or simply enjoying the tranquility of a quiet moment. Stoicism, thus, ensures that even as we step into a phase often associated with loss - we gain, in the form of deep contentment and serenity.

Stoicism, therefore, is a philosophy of acceptance, contentment, control, and simplicity—an ideal lens to view, navigate, and redefine retirement. It reassures us that even after years of timelines, targets, and tests, there still remain life's lessons to learn, simple joys to uncover, and serenity to be embraced. The wisdom of the Stoics encourages us to embark on this journey with courage, grace, and an open heart, ready to welcome whatever life brings. "Retirement? Bring it on!"

Chapter 3. Impermanence: The Stoic Acceptance of Change

One of the most powerful aspects of Stoic philosophy deals with the acceptance of change and the impermanence of life. Accepting, even embracing, impermanence is one of the most liberating and empowering acts we can undertake. It may appear daunting, especially during retirement, as this phase is often symbolic of ultimate change. Nonetheless, by applying the Stoic wisdom about change, we can navigate this period energetically and happily.

3.1. Embracing Change

Stoicism teaches that all things are transient. The seasons change, civilizations rise and fall, and life constantly moves and evolves. Seneca, a renowned Stoic philosopher, once said, "Everywhere means nowhere: when a person spends all his time in foreign travel, he ends by having many acquaintances, but no friends." This illustrates the importance of being situated and steadfast amid change, focusing on aspects of life that bring substance and meaning rather than seeking constant novelty.

Retirement is a significant change, marking the transition from decades of work and routine to a phase with possible uncertainty. Embracing this change, rather than resisting it, can result in captivating experiences and newfound significance.

3.2. The Greek Concept of Panta Rhei

A cornerstone for understanding the Stoic acceptance of change lies in the ancient Greek phrase "Panta Rhei," or "everything flows." Believed to have originated from Heraclitus, an influential pre-Socratic philosopher, Panta Rhei encapsulates the idea that change is the only constant in life.

Bringing this concept to retirement is constructive and grounding. The concerns surrounding finance, identity, purpose, and more that subtly tie the threads of anxiety around change can be untangled effortlessly. As we flow with the current of life, adapting to the evolving situations, we build resilience and create harmony within ourselves.

3.3. Slowing Down to Accelerate Contentment

In the modern world, change often equates to acceleration and unceasing business. The Stoics approached it differently. They cherished change as the natural order of the world and a constant reminder of the impermanence of everything. Slowing down was not deemed regressive but, instead, it was seen as the path to sensibly comprehend life's changing nature and, thereby, to deeper contentment.

Retirement can be a time of slowing down, a period to savor life in all its richness. Such deceleration allows for the cultivation of deeper relationships, engaging hobbies, and activities that were previously sidelined due to professional commitments.

3.4. Tranquility amidst Change

Stoicism teaches that tranquility is achieved by aligning with the flow of life rather than obstructing it. This view, rooted in accepting change, can be an invigorating and enlightening perspective throughout retirement.

Applying this philosophy enables retirees to constructively navigate the highs and lows of this phase. It may be as simple as adopting a new hobby due to physical constraints or as profound as dealing with the loss of a loved one. The reassurance that change is the only constant can provide tremendous solace during challenging times and also enhance the joy during moments of celebration.

3.5. Handling Loss and Grief

Retirement often brings with it encounters with loss and grief. Stoic philosophy, with its focus on the acceptance of change and impermanence, offers valuable insights into handling these challenging circumstances. Epictetus, a prominent Stoic philosopher, proposed, "Do not seek for things to happen the way you want them to; rather, wish that what happens happen the way it naturally does."

By understanding that loss is a natural part of life, we can learn to endure our grief with grace and come out stronger, enabling us to cherish the moments we have with those still with us. This philosophy empowers us to love fully and genuinely, knowing that change, including loss, is inevitable.

The acceptance of change and understanding its transient nature can transform how we experience retirement. We will then find ourselves surfing on the waves of constant change, relishing every crest and trough, rather than fearing it. For ultimate serenity in retirement, one ought to remember the wise words of Marcus Aurelius, a Stoic emperor, who believed, "The universe is change; life is an opinion." Such a perspective, framed by Stoic wisdom, can ensure a fulfilling retirement, filled with growth, contentment, and tranquility.

Chapter 4. Contentment: A Stoic Approach to Satisfaction and Simplicity

Beyond the lofty ideals of tranquility and virtue that has been so closely intertwined with Stoic philosophy, it also emphasizes the simplicity of life and recognition of the things within our control. Contentment, in its true essence, is very much at the heart of this philosophy, and therefore, fully understanding this will help navigate the journey of retirement with satisfaction and simplicity.

4.1. Understanding Contentment in Stoicism

Within the Stoic philosophy, contentment does not spring from possessing things, but rather, arises from a keen and critical understanding of one's desires, clearing misconceptions and misjudgments, and most importantly, recognizing the ephemeral nature of our existence. In essence, a contented life in Stoicism is about seeking inner peace by accepting the fact that not all things are within our control. By clearly distinguishing between what we can and cannot control and choosing to focus our energy on the former, we can thereby create a realm of peace within ourselves.

Chasing contentment in the external world often leads to a cycle of never-ending wants and needs. This, in turn, tends to bring about dissatisfaction and discontent. Stoics assert that the key to breaking this cycle lies within — it is about resetting the baseline of our desires and cultivating an attitude of gratitude irrespective of our situations.

4.2. The Dichotomy of Control

A primary component of implementing Stoic philosophies into retirement is understanding Epictetus' dichotomy of control. The ancient Greek philosopher emphasized that some things are within our control, while others are not.

The concept is simple: We can control our internal thoughts, beliefs, and actions. We have no control over external events, outcomes, or other people's thoughts or actions. As we navigate through retirement, it's essential to understand this and let go of the need to control everything around us.

The practice of dichotomy of control involves recognizing the variables in each situation, identifying what we can impact, and releasing worry about elements beyond our reach. Once we realign our focus, thoughts, and actions towards factors within our control, we create an internal environment of peace and contentment.

4.3. Simplicity and Satisfaction

Engaging with simplicity is a fundamental aspect of Stoic practice, marking a clear path to contentment. Seneca wisely advised, "It is not the man who has too little, but the man who craves more, that is poor." Here, our needs and wants are drastically reduced to simple basics, ridding ourselves of unnecessary desires and clutter.

Retirement is the perfect phase to embrace simplicity. The drive for career advancements, financial growth, and social prestige often dilutes as we step into this phase. With a shift in life's priorities, retirement allows for the elimination of complex routines and commitments. It opens pathways to a deeper connection with oneself, nature, and loved ones, contributing to a more satisfying and fulfilling life experience.

An elemental part of living a simple life involves appreciating the ordinary miracles of every day. Watch the sunrise, enjoy a good book, spend time nurturing a garden - the simplicity in these activities often results in profound satisfaction and contentment. Intentional living by focusing on present moments and cherishing small victories brings unexpected joy and satisfaction.

4.4. Transitioning to New Normals with Grace

Retirement is often accompanied by significant changes – changes that can stir feelings of uncertainty and discomfort. Stoicism prompts us to embrace these transitions with grace and equanimity, viewing them not as hindrances but as natural progressions of life.

External circumstances, as per Stoicism, shouldn't define our happiness or contentment. The focus should instead be on responses and attitudes towards these changes. Recognizing that change is a given in the grand scheme of things, and maintaining composure and tranquility amidst these changes, can lead to enduring contentment.

The Stoic philosophy teaches us that retirement is not a period of loss, but rather an opportunity to gain new experiences, insights, and perspectives. By shifting our attitudes and perceptions this way, we can find that retirement is indeed liberating and contentment is truly attainable.

In conclusion, Stoicism presents a time-tested pathway to effective retirement — a path that leads to contentment, simplicity, and satisfaction. As opposed to viewing retirement as a daunting journey that marks the end, Stoicism encourages you to shift perspective; see it as the beginning of a journey towards self-discovery and satisfaction. After all, retirement is not just an end of a job. If navigated wisely, it is a gateway to contentment, ideal for embracing peace and discovering new dimensions of life.

Chapter 5. Freedom in Retirement: Stoic Insights

Living in retirement offers an unparalleled sense of freedom. For the Stoics, this word carried far more profound implications. It signified autonomy, the ability to think and act independently, and self-governance. Let's delve into the wonderment of freedom in retirement through the refined lens of Stoic philosophy.

5.1. Embracing Autonomy and Independence

Stoics understood freedom in the context of control over decisions, actions, and reactions. This idea is often shown in the philosophy of Epictetus, who taught, "We should always be asking ourselves: 'Is this something that is, or is not, in my control?'" A retired individual has control over their choices in numerous areas of life, presenting an opportunity to consciously steer the direction of well-being and day-to-day satisfaction.

As per the Stoic philosophy, life outcomes depend on own actions and not external circumstances. For retirees, the autonomy means relishing the opportunity to dictate the pace, shape the day, and select the activities fitting their lifestyle objectives. Hence, freedom in retirement is not just about not having to work anymore, but it's about having the independence to make decisions, explore uncharted territories, and express oneself fully, without hindrances.

5.2. Life Skills for Reclaiming Control

Stoicism encourages cognitive resilience, a skill retirees might need while dealing with unpredictable circumstances. Stoics articulate that we control our reactions and actions, not the events around us. In the context of retirement, this might mean being content with a modest lifestyle due to a limited pension, or adopting a robust mindset while confronting health issues.

For building resilience, Stoics devised practical mental exercises. One core strategy was 'premeditatio malorum,' which involved imagining worst-case scenarios to reduce anxiety and stress. As a retiree, regularly practising this technique might involve anticipating potential health issues, financial instability or feelings of loneliness, and preparing oneself emotionally to confront such situations calmly.

5.3. Cultivating Self-Governance

Per Stoicism, freedom doesn't lie merely within economic independence or leisure opportunities. It lies in mastering oneself, becoming self-sufficient in the context of emotional states. Stoic philosophers like Seneca emphasized tranquillity of mind as the pathway to real freedom. Hence, the retiree motivated by Stoic wisdom would aim to cultivate self-governance, ensuring peace and harmony within oneself.

Serenity in retirement comes with balance and mental agility. Stoics taught that freedom is only achieved when one knows exactly what they can control and what they can't, and therefore they focus their energy on that which is within their reach. This sense of self-governance in retired life allows people to navigate the highs and lows with more serenity, taking comfort in the understanding that external circumstances don't define inner peace.

5.4. Redefining Boundaries

The need to set boundaries doesn't disappear with retirement. However, these boundaries take on a new form. For many, it's about deriving a balance between 'doing' and 'being.' Stoics especially valued the state of 'being,' implying a contentment with the present moment, with what is.

Retirement affords the individual an invaluable luxury - time. Free from the stress of a hectic work-life, retirees can now wholly concentrate on fully experiencing their life. Stoic philosophy provides a framework to appreciate life as a series of present moments, instead of a saga driven by past regrets or future anxieties. By setting boundaries around what matters, retirees can learn to anchor themselves more firmly in the 'now' and live with authenticity and mindfulness.

To conclude, freedom in retirement - as seen through a Stoic's lens - is much more than a freedom 'from' working life; it is a freedom 'to' create, explore, and, most importantly, enjoy the tranquillity of one's mind. As retirees lean into Stoic wisdom, they can approach this phase of life with ready adaptability, careful resilience, enthusiastic exploration, and serene self-governance, steering towards an enriching and fulfilling retired life.

Chapter 6. Focusing on the Present: The Stoic's Guide to Mindfulness

Whether you're just getting your feet wet with retirement or you've been at it for a bit, you've undoubtedly heard the phrase "live in the present." For some, this might evoke mental images of peaceful yogis in meditation, while for others, it may sound like trendy pop psychology. But the concept of focusing on the present is far from a modern invention; in fact, it's an essential principle in Stoic philosophy. So, let's dive in to discover how mindfulness, as advocated by Stoicism, can be a valuable tool in your retirement journey.

6.1. The Core of Stoic Mindfulness

To appreciate the Stoic view of mindfulness, it's essential to understand the basic tenets of this philosophy. Stoicism urges us to focus on what's within our control; essentially, our thoughts, beliefs, and reactions. External events, according to the Stoics, are not within our sphere of influence and should therefore not be a source of distress.

Mindfulness, in this context, refers to the concentration on our immediate experiences, thoughts, and emotions, anchoring ourselves in the present instead of worrying about the past or the future. This active engagement with the present moment is also known as 'prosoche,' deriving from the original Greek term utilized by the Stoics.

6.2. Cultivating Attention and Presence

The first step to achieving mindfulness is actively paying attention to our engagement with the world around us. It's about noticing the taste of your morning coffee rather than gulping it down while planning your day.

In retirement, there might be a tendency to rehash past experiences or brood over future uncertainties. However, Staic mindfulness asks us to resist this urge. Instead, it prompts us to immerse ourselves in the 'now,' valuing the interaction, the task, or even the silence that is presently enveloping us.

6.3. Appreciating the Value of Moments

Experience is like a mosaic, made up of tiny, individual moments. The value of a moment when considered in isolation might seem minuscule. However, when viewed as a part of this grand mosaic of life, each moment gains immense significance.

This realization is at the heart of Stoic mindfulness. Stoics believed in the power and inherent value of the present. Their philosophy encourages us to find beauty and significance in every moment, no matter how mundane.

6.4. Practical Steps to Enhancing Mindfulness

Developing mindfulness is a journey that requires practice. Thankfully, Stoicism provides some practical steps that can help fortify this skill in your day-to-day life.

Firstly, engage in self-reflection. The end of the day is a great time to reflect on your actions, thoughts, and feelings. What elicited strong emotions in you? Were you able to remain in the present, or did your mind wander?

Next, maintain a personal journal. This is an invaluable tool to track progress and identify patterns that disrupt mindfulness. Stoic philosophers, like Marcus Aurelius, also compiled their thoughts in a journal, eventually resulting in classics like 'Meditations.'

Finally, indulge in meditation. This practice helps train your mind to focus on the present, allowing you to sift between useful and unhelpful thoughts.

6.5. Embracing Stoic Mindfulness in Retirement

Embracing Stoic mindfulness in retirement can help cultivate a sense of calm and fulfillment. It assists in demystifying retirement anxieties, such as the fear of inactivity or worries about the future, by rooting your perspective firmly in the present moment.

A stoic-minded retiree appreciates the 'now,' reveling in day-to-day activities, celebrating the mundane, and finding joy in interactions. Stoic mindfulness, therefore, can become the compass guiding retirees towards peace and contentment.

6.6. Summing It Up

The Stoic's Guide to Mindfulness in retirement is all about honing in on the present, keeping your mind clear of the clutters of past regrets and future fears. By directing your focus towards the 'now,' you can truly embark on a fulfilling journey of inner peace and contentment. Remember, every moment holds an opportunity for mindful engagement. As the Stoic philosopher Seneca once said, "The whole future lies in uncertainty: live immediately." In retirement, you have an abundance of 'immediately' to live. So, immerse yourself in the present and let the journey of Stoic mindfulness unfold.

Chapter 7. Resilience: Handling Retirement Challenges the Stoic Way

Within retirement's vast expanse, it's inevitable that one will encounter navigation hurdles, ranging from financial constraints and health problems to the disorienting freedom of suddenly abundant leisure time. Stoicism suggests that these are not just challenges but opportunities for inner growth, reinforcing one's resilience. In this section, we'll explore these challenges from a Stoic perspective and construct a roadmap to cultivate resilience.

7.1. Understanding Resilience: The Stoic Way

According to Stoic philosophy, resilience is not a mere attribute but a way of life. It is, in essence, the capacity to endure adversity while maintaining inner peace. Stoicism teaches not to shirk away from adversity, but to welcome it as a platform for spiritual and mental growth. Here, Epictetus' wise words ring true, "It's not what happens to you, but how you react to it that matters."

Resilience doesn't mean you won't face hardship or feel pain; it means that despite the difficulties, you will persist. You will understand that our time on earth is transient, and everything, both comfort and discomfort, is fleeting. You realize, deeply and irrevocably, that life's uncontrollable factors are outside your realm of influence, and what you do control are your responses.

7.2. Embracing Discomfort: Chasing Rainbows within the Clouds

Imagine a life without challenges. Would there be opportunities for growth, or would we stagnate in monotonous comfort? Stoicism posits that adversity is an indispensable tutor, molding our character, imparting lifelong lessons. Seneca, the Roman Stoic philosopher, said, "Difficulties strengthen the mind, as labor does the body."

Embrace the discomforts of retirement as opportunities to test your mettle. Missing your old life? Engage in Stoic reflection and practice negative visualization. This strategy requires envisioning the worst-case scenario, such as not having retired at all, still being caught up in the stressors of professional life. Such reflection helps appreciate the current circumstances more and dispels unfounded fears around retirement.

7.3. Cultivating Mindfulness: Being in the 'Stoic Now'

Retirement brings ample leisure time, which can initially be disorienting. Here, it's helpful to cultivate 'present-focused mindfulness.' Mindfulness is not just a Buddhist concept; it holds equal significance in Stoicism, reminding us that the only 'time' we truly have is 'now.'

Marcus Aurelius, the Roman Emperor and a practicing Stoic, wrote, "Confine yourself to the present." Stoic mindfulness helps you to stay grounded in the present, taking each moment as it comes, without excessive worry about future uncertainties or past regrets. Cultivating this attitude keeps distress at bay while helping you savour simple joys.

7.4. Handling Health Issues with Grace

For some, health issues can mar the tranquility of retirement. Yet, from a Stoic point of view, while we cannot always control our body's ailing, we can control our reaction to it. The key here is to understand the dichotomy of control, a cornerstone of Stoic philosophy.

Aging bodies will inevitably present challenges, but we can control how we approach these challenges. Do we lament the loss of youth, or do we gracefully accept aging as a natural life progression? Adapting a Stoic attitude towards health can not only lessen fears and frustrations around health deterioration but also allow us to approach medical procedures and lifestyle modifications necessary for healthy aging with calm acceptance.

7.5. Navigating Financial Resources

Lastly, financial concerns are often coupled with retirement. Here, it's useful to recall the Stoic principle of 'preferred indifferents.' Remember, the Stoics did not advocate poverty, but they understood that wealth could neither guarantee virtue nor peace. It's about making the best of what one has and not lamenting what one doesn't.

The Stoics would advocate prudent budgeting, strategic planning, and selective spending to stretch the retirement income. They would also encourage finding joy in simple, cost-effective activities. Stoicism equips you to face financial adversities with equanimity, making us understand that richness lies not in material possessions but in internal peace and contentment.

Stoic resilience, thus, empowers you to navigate retirement challenges not just with calmness but with optimism, grace, and a sense of purpose. So, march forth into the landscape of retirement wielding your Stoic shield of resilience, transforming supposed hardships into waypoints in your journey towards inner peace.

Chapter 8. Retirement Relationships: A Stoic Perspective on Friendship and Family

Friendship and family relationships figure largely in retirement, their dynamics changing considerably with the onset of this new life stage. Stoic philosophy, with its core tenets embracing acceptance, peace, and the pursuit of virtue, can provide invaluable insights on how to navigate, maintain, and even strengthen these bonds.

8.1. Embracing Change in Relationships

Retirement signals a significant shift in lifestyle, often altering the framework of our relationships. As work-related commitments wane, one finds themselves with an abundance of time to invest in personal relationships. However, this is not always easy. The increased proximity to family and friends can lead to friction due to a change in dynamics or the surfacing of long-dormant issues.

The Stoic approach encourages acceptance of reality as it is. Epictetus, a prominent Stoic philosopher, wrote, "It is not things that disturb us, but our interpretation of their significance." In the context of relationships, this means understanding and accepting that change is an intrinsic part of life, and the shifts in post-retirement relationships are no exception.

Focus on controllable aspects. You cannot control how others behave or react, but you can control your own perceptions, reactions, and attitudes. Accept the shifting dynamics, adapt without resisting, and forge ahead with openness and a willingness to constructively work towards harmonious relationships.

8.2. A Stoic View of Family Relationships

Stoicism's central theme, the cultivation of virtue and inner wisdom, finds invaluable application in navigating family relationships in retirement. Pivoting towards a focus on what matters, you can choose to engage more deeply, retain peace when there is discord, and respect the individual paths of your loved ones.

Marcus Aurelius, another renowned Stoic philosopher, explained that we should engage with others from a place of understanding and compassion. Each person, including family members, has their own journey and life experiences that contribute to their beliefs and behavior. Recognize this diversity, appreciate it, and where there are differences, strive to understand rather than judge or control.

By adopting a non-reactive stance, inspired by Stoic equanimity, you can nurture relationships with a sense of calm. This is essentially the pursuit of tranquillity, the ability to maintain inner peace despite stormy or stressful events around us.

8.3. Stoic Friendship in Retirement

In contrast to family ties, friendships in retirement can be more complex. Beyond shared workplace experiences, sustaining these bonds can be challenging. Yet, friendships, especially in retirement, can contribute significantly to emotional health and overall happiness.

The Stoic perspective on this could be to reevaluate friendships based on virtues of trust, mutual respect, and shared values. It encourages releasing friendships that feel draining or discordant with your values, providing space for more fulfilling relationships.

Seneca, the stoic sage, expressed that friendship is about resonating on the same moral and intellectual wavelength. He reminds us to engage in friendships not for utility or pleasure alone, but for shared virtue.

8.4. Developing New Relationships in Retirement

Building new relationships isn't exclusive to the younger generation; it's equally applicable to retirees. Inculcating a curiosity about and openness to new interactions can result in fruitful acquaintances or even precious friendships.

Practicing Stoicism, you cultivate indifference towards societal or self-imposed age limitations. Stoics remind us of the value of a beginners' mindset - adopting an attitude of openness, eagerness, and a lack of preconceptions when approaching life. This approach simplifies the process of making new connections in retirement.

From a Stoic viewpoint, one is drawn to relationships based on virtue and shared interests. Take this opportunity to explore new avenues, participate in community activities, or delve deeper into your hobbies. By authentically engaging in activities you love, you will likely find others who share your interests leading to the formation of enriching new relationships.

8.5. Nurturing Self-relationship

Stoicism, at its core, emphasizes self-improvement and personal virtue. In retirement, time with oneself increases, and the relationship you hold with yourself comes to the forefront.

Self-reflection, an essential practice in Stoicism, guides you to evaluate your actions, thoughts, and nature regularly. Practice this self-dialogue to understand your values better, rectify errors, and consistently steer yourself towards virtue. This also encompass acceptance and forgiveness for oneself, essential for self-growth and peace.

Embrace the solitude that retirement often brings. Use it to engage with yourself, declutter your mind, and realign your values and actions. Stoics often spoke of the virtue of solitude in fostering self-growth and attaining tranquillity.

With these Stoic strategies, redefining and revitalizing relationships in retirement is achievable, providing you with the tools needed to navigate this life stage with serenity and contentment. Lines of communication will open, bonds will strengthen, and new relationships will flourish, leading to a more fulfilled and peaceful retirement.

Remember, as Seneca said, "As is a tale, so is life: not how long it is, but how good it is, is what matters." In relationships too, it's not about how many we have but how good they are that leads to contentment in retirement.

Chapter 9. Maintaining Wellness: Physical Health and Stoic Philosophy

Stoic philosophy guides us to understand that while we may not control all the circumstances, we can greatly influence our health outcomes by the perspective, choices, and actions we employ. As we look into maintaining physical health during retirement, let's explore how Stoic insights can equip us with the mental toolkit to face this challenge head-on.

9.1. The Importance of Physical Health

Optimizing physical health plays a pivotal role in the quality of life during retirement. Regular activity not only strengthens the body, but also fosters cognitive health, improves mood, and extends healthy lifespan. As the words of the famous Stoic philosopher, Socrates, suggest, "No citizen has a right to be an amateur in the matter of physical training...What a disgrace it is for a man to grow old without ever seeing the beauty and strength of which his body is capable."

No matter our age, we can strive to realize our body's potential for strength and vitality because wellness is not merely the absence of disease, but a dynamic process of change and growth.

9.2. Stoicism and Physical Health

Stoicism values virtue, wisdom, and mindfulness. It reminds us that our bodies are the vessels that carry our souls – and thus, deserve care and respect. Practicing Stoicism encourages us to focus on what we can control: our attitudes, actions, and responses. This principle can be readily applied to physical health in retirement.

Rather, being Stoic can mean taking sensible, practical steps towards maintaining, or even improving, physical health. Healthy nutrition, regular exercise, and routine healthcare check-ups are completely in our control. It's essential to realize the value of these aspects and to work them into our daily routine to improve our well-being as we age.

But how does one train oneself to adopt and persist with these Stoic health practices, particularly when age or infirmity makes them difficult?

9.3. Developing Discipline and Consistency

Stoicism teaches us a great deal about discipline, reinforcing that it is through committed practice, not instinct or immediate gratification, that we cultivate virtue. Similarly, maintaining physical health in retirement necessitates discipline, consistency, and an unwavering commitment to our wellness.

Developing discipline can begin with small, daily habits. These might include a daily walk around the block, switching to healthier food choices, or keeping up-to-date with medical appointments. Each positive action, however small, is a step towards improved physical health. As Seneca once said, "It does not matter how slowly you go as long as you do not stop."

9.4. Adapting to Physical Changes

Just as a river's flow adapts to the shape and form of the land, we must adapt to the inevitable changes that aging brings. Marcus

Aurelius often noted the impermanence of all things, and this equally applies to our physical state.

Aging inevitably brings changes, some of which might include decreased mobility, reduced energy levels, or increased susceptibility to illness. However, the Stoic perspective would encourage acceptance of these changes and adaptation to new routines suitable to this period of life.

Take, for instance, the arena of exercise. If you once ran marathons but now find running to be a difficult feat, you might consider alternatives like walking, swimming, or gentle yoga. These activities can keep you active, help maintain strength and joint flexibility, and improve your mood - just as effectively as running.

The same approach of adaptability applies to nutrition. With age, nutritional needs change. The importance of balanced, nutrient-rich diets suitable for your age cannot be overstressed. Such proactive adaptation helps create a symbiosis with our changing physical state, rather than fight it.

9.5. Embracing Mindfulness for Wellness

A key tenet of Stoicism, mindfulness, emphasises being present in the moment, aware and focused on the task at hand. From a physical health perspective, it can be as simple as paying attention to our bodies' signals of hunger and fullness, stress, and fatigue. Being responsive to these signals lets us detect and address wellness issues early on.

Forming a mindful connection with our bodies can also help us recover from and cope with illness or health setbacks better. We begin to understand our body's unique rhythms and limits and can make informed decisions that respect our individual needs.

It's heartening to know that as long as we are here to experience the world, we possess the potential to improve our health and wellness to some degree. While the physical journey of each individual varies, it is our response to it that is truly within our control. Remember that retirement is a golden opportunity to focus on wellness and longevity, to take the time to listen to our bodies and treat them with the care and respect they deserve. Employing the principles of Stoic philosophy can guide us through this journey. Let's live those wise words from Marcus Aurelius: "Do not act as if you had ten thousand years to throw away. Death stands at your elbow. Be good for something while you're alive and able."

Chapter 10. The Stoic's Approach to Lifelong Learning in Retirement

Learning and personal development don't stop when we retire; they merely take a new direction. Stoic philosophy offers valuable insights and practices that can profoundly enhance our lifelong learning experiences as we navigate the sea of retirement.

10.1. Embracing Continuous Growth

Stoicism emphasizes the importance of focusing on continuous self-improvement and not getting complacent with what one already knows. This virtue of embracing growth is more relevant than ever in retirement, where one has the time and freedom to explore new domains of knowledge. Seneca, a prominent Stoic, once wrote, "As long as you live, keep learning how to live." This timeless piece of wisdom is a call to immerse oneself in continuous learning and exploration throughout life, including during retirement.

10.2. The Stoic Virtue of Wisdom

In Stoicism, wisdom is more than just the acquisition of knowledge. It is also about developing the judgment to choose and act correctly. As retirees, we have the unique opportunity to not only learn new things but also deepen our understanding of life. Spending time reflecting on one's experiences, reading philosophy, history, or any subject of interest, can generate insights that serve to better equip us for the challenges of life.

10.3. Lifelong Learning as Emotional Resilience

Stoicism provides a perspective that can enable one to engage in lifelong learning as a means of cultivating emotional resilience. Retirement can sometimes lead to feelings of irrelevance or lack of purpose. Engaging in continuous learning and personal development, however, can imbue life with purpose and meaning, making one resilient to such emotional challenges. Epictetus suggested, "It's not what happens to you, but how you react to it that matters." Lifelong learning can be a powerful tool to channel one's reactions in a positive direction.

10.4. A Stoic's Guide to Choosing What to Learn

A critical piece of Stoic wisdom is directing our focus on what we can control, and ignore what we can't. This principle holds true when choosing what to learn during retirement. It's not about following trends or what others are doing but about pursuing subjects that pique your interest, develop your character, and add value to your life.

10.5. Learning from Adversity

Another Stoic principle useful in lifelong learning is the ability to learn from adversity. Retirement can come with its fair share of changes and challenges that might destabilize one's equilibrium temporarily. However, Stoics see adversity as an excellent opportunity for learning. As Marcus Aurelius wisely reflected, "The impediment to action advances action. What stands in the way becomes the way." Hence, it's not about avoiding difficulties but navigating through them, turning adversities into opportunities for growth and learning.

10.6. Learning in Savoring the Present

Stoicism underscores the significance of living in the present moment. To truly learn something, one must be fully present in the experience without being chained by past regrets or future anxieties. Practicing mindfulness in learning pursuits during retirement can deepen understanding and enhance enjoyment.

10.7. Applying Stoic Wisdom to Real Life

Merely acquiring knowledge is not enough. The application of that acquired wisdom to real-life situations is where the true value lies. This is where your own wealth of personal experience can be a valuable assistant in your retirement learning journey.

In conclusion, the Stoic's approach to lifelong learning in retirement is about framing this phase as an opportunity for self-improvement in wisdom and virtue, as well as resilience. It's about proactively choosing what to learn, learning from difficulties, savoring the present, and applying what we learn to enhance the quality of our lives. As Stoicism teaches us, retirement isn't an ending but the beginning of a new learning journey. It's time to leverage Stoic wisdom to make this journey truly fruitful.

Chapter 11. Conclusion: Embracing the Serenity of Retirement with Stoicism

In contemplating the serenity of retirement through the lens of Stoicism, we find a comforting embrace of change and aging, graceful acceptance of the past's irreversibility, and a profound understanding of the present's value. This chapter serves as the harmonious finale to our exploration, presenting the ultimate condensation of Stoic wisdom applicable to bidding our professional lives adieu and welcoming the tranquil ambiance of retirement.

11.1. The Stoic Embrace of Change and Aging

Stoic philosophy views change as a natural and inevitable aspect of existence. All things in the universe, including our bodies and minds, operate by the laws of nature. Aging, then, is not an aberration to be denied or hidden but an expected outcome of the passage of time. Marcus Aurelius, a prominent Stoic philosopher, writes in his Meditations, "Time is a sort of river of passing events, and strong is its current."

Retirement signals a significant change, both in terms of career and identity. Yet, in the flux of life, a Stoic understands this transition as a stage, not a terminus. Redefining one's self apart from a job title or professional role is not just a choice but a necessity. Epictetus advises us that resisting nature's course leads to discomfort: "Do not seek to have events happen as you want them to, but instead want them to happen as they do happen, and your life will go well."

11.2. Accepting the Past and Maximizing the Present

To enjoy retirement serenity, a key tool offered by Stoicism is the concept of 'Amor Fati'– love of fate. Essentially, adopting this mindset means accepting past events–whether they were in or out of our control–as ingredients necessary for the person we are today. Stoic philosopher Seneca advises us not to dwell on the past or worry about the future, insisting instead that we concentrate on making the most of the present moment.

Understanding and valuing the present doesn't mean one should be idle in retirement. On the contrary, a Stoic maximizes the present moment, seizing opportunities for continuous learning, involvement in activities or causes close to one's heart - contributing toward living meaningfully.

11.3. Living a Virtuous and Fulfilled Life

Stoicism underscores the importance of virtues such as courage, wisdom, justice, and temperance. These provide the foundation for living a life of composure, purpose, and satisfaction. Retirement offers the perfect setting to prioritize these virtues as we have the time and space for introspection and self-improvement.

In retirement, we can embody courage by confronting new challenges, from learning a new skill to facing the realities of aging. Wisdom manifests in accepting the reality of our situations and adopting a balanced viewpoint about life's pleasures and pressures. A sense of justice reveals itself through involvement in voluntary initiatives, while temperance keeps a firm check on excessive indulgence, encourages a balanced lifestyle, and promotes longevity.

11.4. Engaging with the Community

A retired life steeped in Stoic doctrine is not one of isolation but involves active community engagement. Engaging with the community in meaningful ways, contributing to causes you care for, or sharing the wisdom of your years with younger generations, compounds the joy of your golden years.

The vision of Stoicism in retirement crystallizes to create a picture of serenity, a life stage filled with contentment, resilience, and a sense of fulfillment. Arguably, it's more than just a method of navigating the challenges of retirement - it's the philosophy we need to live our best lives. Stepping into retirement armed with the wisdom and guidance of Stoic philosophy will not only redefine this often-misunderstood stage of life but also nurture an attitude of acceptance, engagement, and delight.

In sum, Stoicism's application to retirement liberates us from common fears surrounding this life stage. By removing the dread and anxiety, we pave the path for retirement to become an opportunity for wholesome enrichment, self-realization, and contentment.

By the end of this journey, you'll have the fortitude to gleefully welcome retirement, embodying the Stoic spirit of courage, wisdom, justice, and temperance. As we cast our gaze forward, equipped with the invaluable guidance of Stoicism, we may confidently echo Seneca's words, "As is a tale, so is life: not how long it is, but how good it is, is what matters." Indeed, let's pour our energies not into worrying about the length of our retirement years but into ensuring that these years are filled with purpose, serenity, and joy. Retirement? Certainly, bring it on!

www.ingramcontent.com/pod-product-compliance
Lightning Source LLC
Chambersburg PA
CBHW072221290526
45794CB00007B/2832